Teach Your Child to Read

300 Short Easy Sentences

English - Spanish

Name

I Can...

- [ ] read the 1st sentence.
- [ ] read the 2nd sentence.
- [ ] make a sentence from a picture.
- [ ] color a picture.
- [ ] Draw a picture.

The frog is going to a party.

La rana va a una fiesta.

The happy frog is wearing a green hat.

La rana feliz lleva un sombrero verde.

Name

I Can...

- ☐ read the 1st sentence.
- ☐ read the 2nd sentence.
- ☐ make a sentence from a picture.
- ☐ color a picture.
- ☐ Draw a picture.

Owl likes to read big books.

A Owl le gusta leer libros grandes.

A smart owl is reading an alphabet book.

Un búho inteligente está leyendo un libro del alfabeto.

Name 

I Can...

- [ ] read the 1st sentence.
- [ ] read the 2nd sentence.
- [ ] make a sentence from a picture.
- [ ] color a picture.
- [ ] Draw a picture.

Come on! The ice cream truck is here!

¡Venga! ¡El camión de helados está aquí!

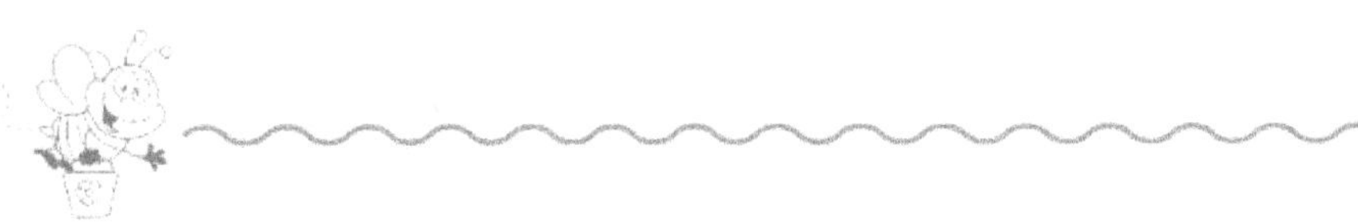

He is driving a big icecream truck.

Él conduce un gran camión de helados.

Name

I Can...

- [ ] read the 1st sentence.
- [ ] read the 2nd sentence.
- [ ] make a sentence from a picture.
- [ ] color a picture.
- [ ] Draw a picture.

Dragons are very friendly and have scales on their backs.

Los dragones son muy amigables y tienen escamas en la espalda.

The dragon is waving his hand.

El dragón está agitando su mano.

Name

I Can...

- [ ] read the 1st sentence.
- [ ] read the 2nd sentence.
- [ ] make a sentence from a picture.
- [ ] color a picture.
- [ ] Draw a picture.

This ram lives in the farmhouse.

Este carnero vive en la granja.

 ～～～～～～～～～～～～～～～～～～～

Ram has a large horn and fluffy wool.

Ram tiene un cuerno grande y lana esponjosa.

Name ___________

I Can...

- [ ] read the 1st sentence.
- [ ] read the 2nd sentence.
- [ ] make a sentence from a picture.
- [ ] color a picture.
- [ ] Draw a picture.

The bunny likes to eat carrots.

Al conejito le gusta comer zanahorias.

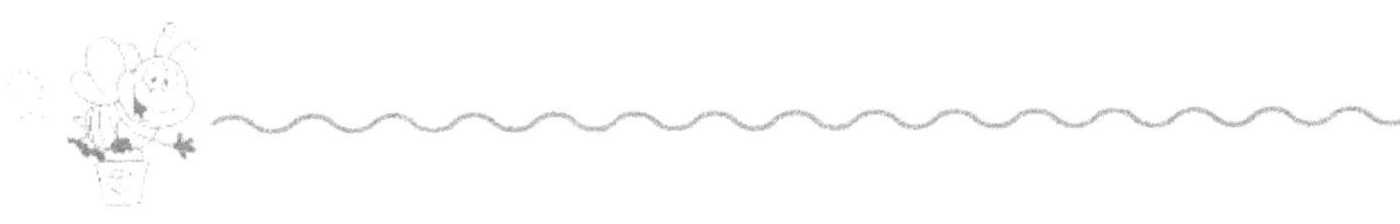

Rabbit thinks that the juicy orange carrot looks yummy.

Rabbit piensa que la zanahoria naranja jugosa se ve deliciosa.

Name

I Can...

- [ ] read the 1st sentence.
- [ ] read the 2nd sentence.
- [ ] make a sentence from a picture.
- [ ] color a picture.
- [ ] Draw a picture.

The clown likes to give out balloons to little kids.

Al payaso le gusta repartir globos a los niños pequeños.

Funny, Mr. Clown is giving away colorful balloons.

Es curioso, el Sr. Payaso está regalando globos de colores.

Name

I Can...

- [ ] read the 1st sentence.
- [ ] read the 2nd sentence.
- [ ] make a sentence from a picture.
- [ ] color a picture.
- [ ] Draw a picture.

The clown is juggling balls for his performance.

El payaso está haciendo malabares con pelotas para su actuación.

Talented, Mr. Clown is juggling five red balls.

Talentoso, Mr. Clown está haciendo malabarismos con cinco bolas rojas.

Name 

I Can...

- [ ] read the 1st sentence.
- [ ] read the 2nd sentence.
- [ ] make a sentence from a picture.
- [ ] color a picture.
- [ ] Draw a picture.

The Easter Bunny is going to give out chocolate eggs.

El conejito de pascua va a repartir huevos de chocolate.

The rabbit goes out to buy more orange carrots.

El conejo sale a comprar más zanahorias anaranjadas.

Name

I Can...

- [ ] read the 1st sentence.
- [ ] read the 2nd sentence.
- [ ] make a sentence from a picture.
- [ ] color a picture.
- [ ] Draw a picture.

The pencil is drawing a zig-zag line.

El lápiz está dibujando una línea en zig-zag.

The Pencil is saying hello to you.

El lápiz te está saludando.

Name

I Can...

- [ ] read the 1st sentence.
- [ ] read the 2nd sentence.
- [ ] make a sentence from a picture.
- [ ] color a picture.
- [ ] Draw a picture.

The pencil put on a big smile and went to work.

El lápiz puso una gran sonrisa y se fue a trabajar.

The Pencil is leaving to go on a long relaxing vacation.

The Pencil se va para tomar unas vacaciones largas y relajantes.

Name

I Can...

- [ ] read the 1st sentence.
- [ ] read the 2nd sentence.
- [ ] make a sentence from a picture.
- [ ] color a picture.
- [ ] Draw a picture.

This snowman is my friend, and he is a helper of Santa.

Este muñeco de nieve es mi amigo, y él es un ayudante de Santa.

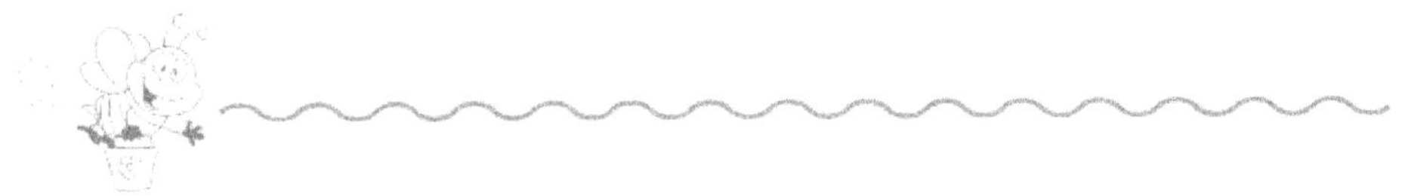

Mr. Snowman is celebrating Christmas by the decorated tree.

El Sr. Snowman está celebrando la Navidad junto al árbol decorado.

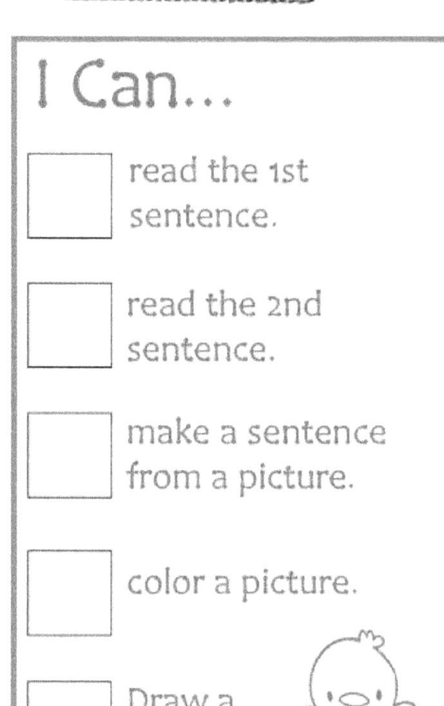

The octopus is working as a chef and serving food.

El pulpo está trabajando como chef y sirve comida.

Chef Octopus is serving a delicious turkey dinner.

El chef Octopus está sirviendo una deliciosa cena de pavo.

14

I Can...

- [ ] read the 1st sentence.
- [ ] read the 2nd sentence.
- [ ] make a sentence from a picture.
- [ ] color a picture.
- [ ] Draw a picture.

Santa is happy.

Santa esta feliz.

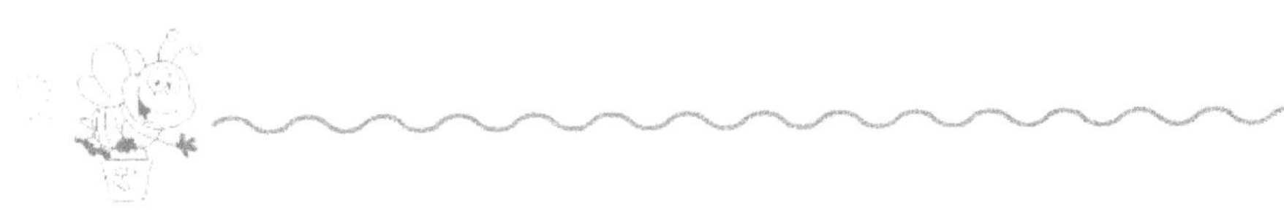

Santa Claus is giving extraordinary presents to excited kids.

Papá Noel está dando regalos extraordinarios a niños entusiasmados.

Name

I Can...

- [ ] read the 1st sentence.
- [ ] read the 2nd sentence.
- [ ] make a sentence from a picture.
- [ ] color a picture.
- [ ] Draw a picture.

The bear likes to eat sweets.

Al oso le gusta comer dulces.

Teddy is licking a red and white candy cane.

Teddy está lamiendo un bastón de caramelo rojo y blanco.

Name 

I Can...

- [ ] read the 1st sentence.
- [ ] read the 2nd sentence.
- [ ] make a sentence from a picture.
- [ ] color a picture.
- [ ] Draw a picture.

The book has a wand.

El libro tiene una varita.

____

The cereal box got a magician set for Christmas.

La caja de cereal tiene un juego de magos para Navidad.

Name

I Can...

- [ ] read the 1st sentence.
- [ ] read the 2nd sentence.
- [ ] make a sentence from a picture.
- [ ] color a picture.
- [ ] Draw a picture.

The bear has a present.

El oso tiene un regalo.

Happy Teddy is opening his box of presents from Santa.

Happy Teddy está abriendo su caja de regalos de Santa.

Name

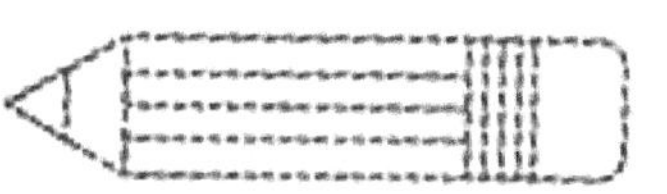

I Can...

- [ ] read the 1st sentence.
- [ ] read the 2nd sentence.
- [ ] make a sentence from a picture.
- [ ] color a picture.
- [ ] Draw a picture.

Santa is going to give out presents.

Santa va a repartir regalos.

Santa is lugging a large brown bag of gifts to his sley.

Santa está cargando una gran bolsa marrón de regalos en su sley.

Name

I Can...

- [ ] read the 1st sentence.
- [ ] read the 2nd sentence.
- [ ] make a sentence from a picture.
- [ ] color a picture.
- [ ] Draw a picture.

I made a snowman.

Hice un muñeco de nieve.

Mr. Snowman is holding a broom and saying goodbye.

El señor Snowman sostiene una escoba y se despide.

Name

I Can...

- [ ] read the 1st sentence.
- [ ] read the 2nd sentence.
- [ ] make a sentence from a picture.
- [ ] color a picture.
- [ ] Draw a picture.

The parrot is colorful.

El loro es colorido.

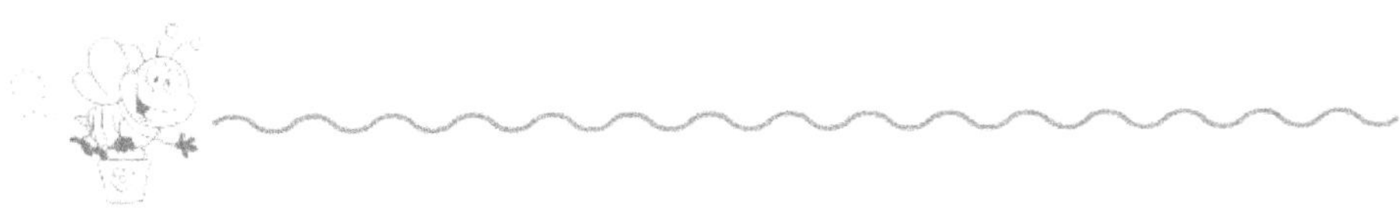

The green parrot came from the forest to the zoo.

El loro verde vino del bosque al zoológico.

Name

I Can...

- [ ] read the 1st sentence.
- [ ] read the 2nd sentence.
- [ ] make a sentence from a picture.
- [ ] color a picture.
- [ ] Draw a picture.

There are a lot of animals.

Hay muchos animales

The animals are happy being together again.

Los animales están felices de estar juntos de nuevo.

Name

I Can...

- [ ] read the 1st sentence.
- [ ] read the 2nd sentence.
- [ ] make a sentence from a picture.
- [ ] color a picture.
- [ ] Draw a picture.

The man is wearing a belt.

El hombre lleva un cinturón.

The carpenter is fixing something.

El carpintero está arreglando algo.

Name ___________

I Can...

- [ ] read the 1st sentence.
- [ ] read the 2nd sentence.
- [ ] make a sentence from a picture.
- [ ] color a picture.
- [ ] Draw a picture.

The rabbit is very young.

El conejo es muy joven.

The magician plays a trick.

El mago juega un truco.

Name

I Can...

- [ ] read the 1st sentence.
- [ ] read the 2nd sentence.
- [ ] make a sentence from a picture.
- [ ] color a picture.
- [ ] Draw a picture.

He has a potion.

El tiene una poción.

The scientist is making a potion.

El científico está haciendo una poción.

Name

I Can...

- [ ] read the 1st sentence.
- [ ] read the 2nd sentence.
- [ ] make a sentence from a picture.
- [ ] color a picture.
- [ ] Draw a picture.

He is wearing sunglasses.

Lleva gafas de sol.

The policeman is mad.

El policía está enojado.

Name

I Can...

- ☐ read the 1st sentence.
- ☐ read the 2nd sentence.
- ☐ make a sentence from a picture.
- ☐ color a picture.
- ☐ Draw a picture.

He has a bucket of paint.

Él tiene un balde de pintura.

He likes to paint.

A él le gusta pintar.

Name

I Can...

- [ ] read the 1st sentence.
- [ ] read the 2nd sentence.
- [ ] make a sentence from a picture.
- [ ] color a picture.
- [ ] Draw a picture.

The man has a hat.

El hombre tiene sombrero.

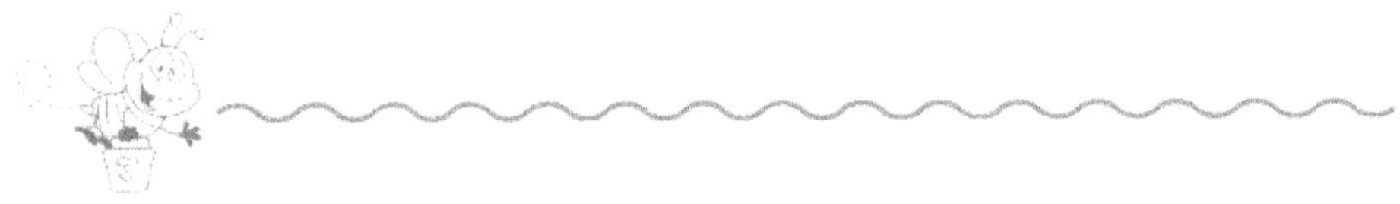

The postman is giving out the mail in the early morning.

El cartero entrega el correo temprano en la mañana.

Name

I Can...

- ☐ read the 1st sentence.
- ☐ read the 2nd sentence.
- ☐ make a sentence from a picture.
- ☐ color a picture.
- ☐ Draw a picture.

He has a walkie talkie.

Él tiene un walkie talkie.

He is going to work with his suitcase.

Él va a trabajar con su maleta.

Name

I Can...

- [ ] read the 1st sentence.
- [ ] read the 2nd sentence.
- [ ] make a sentence from a picture.
- [ ] color a picture.
- [ ] Draw a picture.

He is sleepy.

Tiene sueño.

The delivery man sent us a package.

El repartidor nos envió un paquete.

Name

I Can...

- [ ] read the 1st sentence.
- [ ] read the 2nd sentence.
- [ ] make a sentence from a picture.
- [ ] color a picture.
- [ ] Draw a picture.

He is wearing a bowtie.

Él está usando una corbata de moño.

The waiter is serving juice.

El camarero está sirviendo jugo.

Name

I Can...

- [ ] read the 1st sentence.
- [ ] read the 2nd sentence.
- [ ] make a sentence from a picture.
- [ ] color a picture.
- [ ] Draw a picture.

He has a suitcase.

El tiene una maleta.

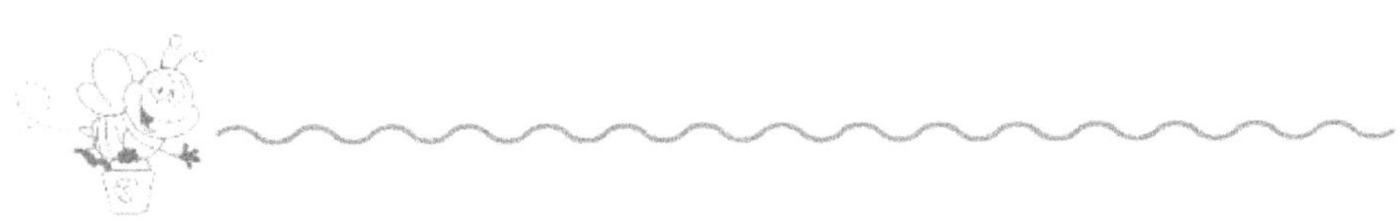

The engineer is holding a wrench.

El ingeniero está sosteniendo una llave inglesa.

Name

I Can...

- [ ] read the 1st sentence.
- [ ] read the 2nd sentence.
- [ ] make a sentence from a picture.
- [ ] color a picture.
- [ ] Draw a picture.

The chef has a napkin.

El chef tiene una servilleta.

The chef serves delicious-looking food.

El chef sirve comida deliciosa.

Name

I Can...

- ☐ read the 1st sentence.
- ☐ read the 2nd sentence.
- ☐ make a sentence from a picture.
- ☐ color a picture.
- ☐ Draw a picture.

The rooster has a big beak.

El gallo tiene un pico grande.

The chicken is saying hello to us.

El pollo nos está saludando.

I Can...

- [ ] read the 1st sentence.
- [ ] read the 2nd sentence.
- [ ] make a sentence from a picture.
- [ ] color a picture.
- [ ] Draw a picture.

The bird is small.

El pájaro es pequeño.

 ~~~~~~~~~~~~~~~~~~~~~~~~~~~~~~~~~~~~~

The chick is on the telephone talking with his friend.

La chica está hablando por teléfono con su amigo.

Name

I Can...

- [ ] read the 1st sentence.
- [ ] read the 2nd sentence.
- [ ] make a sentence from a picture.
- [ ] color a picture.
- [ ] Draw a picture.

That is my ring.

Ese es mi anillo.

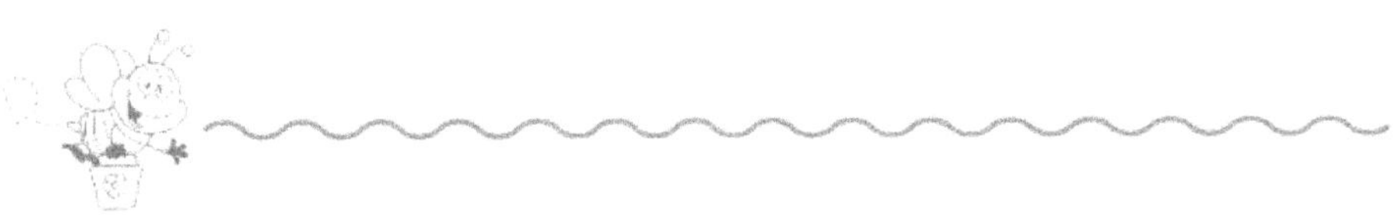

That is a beautiful ring.

Ese es un hermoso anillo.

Name

I Can...

- [ ] read the 1st sentence.
- [ ] read the 2nd sentence.
- [ ] make a sentence from a picture.
- [ ] color a picture.
- [ ] Draw a picture.

The duck has three eggs.

El pato tiene tres huevos.

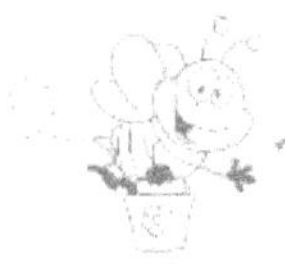

The duck has a big nose.

El pato tiene una nariz grande.

Name

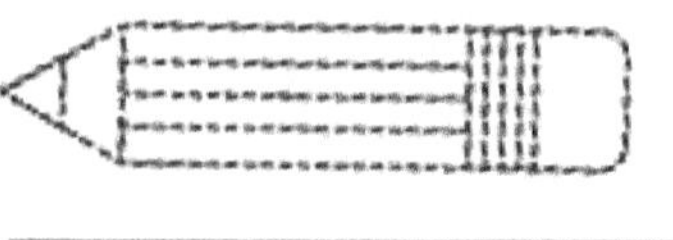

I Can...

- [ ] read the 1st sentence.
- [ ] read the 2nd sentence.
- [ ] make a sentence from a picture.
- [ ] color a picture.
- [ ] Draw a picture.

The swan is beautiful.

El cisne es hermoso

The graceful swan is striding through the water.

El elegante cisne camina por el agua.

Name

I Can...

- [ ] read the 1st sentence.
- [ ] read the 2nd sentence.
- [ ] make a sentence from a picture.
- [ ] color a picture.
- [ ] Draw a picture.

The girl is wearing a dress.

La niña lleva un vestido.

The maid is cleaning our room.

La criada está limpiando nuestra habitación.

Name

I Can...

- [ ] read the 1st sentence.
- [ ] read the 2nd sentence.
- [ ] make a sentence from a picture.
- [ ] color a picture.
- [ ] Draw a picture.

The boy is running.

El niño esta corriendo.

The little boy was running.

El niño corría.

Name

I Can...

- [ ] read the 1st sentence.
- [ ] read the 2nd sentence.
- [ ] make a sentence from a picture.
- [ ] color a picture.
- [ ] Draw a picture.

He is a musician.

Él es un músico.

He is playing a lively tune on his flute.

Él está tocando una melodía animada en su flauta.

I Can...

- [ ] read the 1st sentence.
- [ ] read the 2nd sentence.
- [ ] make a sentence from a picture.
- [ ] color a picture.
- [ ] Draw a picture.

He looks joyful.

Se ve alegre.

That boy works in a band and plays the drum.

Ese chico trabaja en una banda y toca el tambor.

Name

I Can...

- [ ] read the 1st sentence.
- [ ] read the 2nd sentence.
- [ ] make a sentence from a picture.
- [ ] color a picture.
- [ ] Draw a picture.

The dinosaur is a rock star.

El dinosaurio es una estrella de rock.

The dragon is playing the guitar.

El dragón está tocando la guitarra.

Name

I Can...

- [ ] read the 1st sentence.
- [ ] read the 2nd sentence.
- [ ] make a sentence from a picture.
- [ ] color a picture.
- [ ] Draw a picture.

The nurse helps the doctor.

La enfermera ayuda al médico.

The nurse looks scary, holding a syringe.

La enfermera parece aterradora, sosteniendo una jeringa.

Name _______________ 

I Can...

- [ ] read the 1st sentence.
- [ ] read the 2nd sentence.
- [ ] make a sentence from a picture.
- [ ] color a picture.
- [ ] Draw a picture.

She is wearing a crown.

Ella lleva una corona.

 ∿∿∿∿∿∿∿∿∿∿∿∿∿∿∿∿∿∿∿

The queen bee has a beautiful wand.

La abeja reina tiene una hermosa varita.

Name

I Can...

- [ ] read the 1st sentence.
- [ ] read the 2nd sentence.
- [ ] make a sentence from a picture.
- [ ] color a picture.
- [ ] Draw a picture.

It is orange and black.

Es de color naranja y negro.

The tiger is wearing a bow on its neck.

El tigre lleva un lazo en el cuello.

Name

I Can...

- [ ] read the 1st sentence.
- [ ] read the 2nd sentence.
- [ ] make a sentence from a picture.
- [ ] color a picture.
- [ ] Draw a picture.

The boy is carrying a lot of books.

El niño lleva muchos libros.

The boy is carrying so many books!

¡El niño lleva tantos libros!

Name

I Can...

- [ ] read the 1st sentence.
- [ ] read the 2nd sentence.
- [ ] make a sentence from a picture.
- [ ] color a picture.
- [ ] Draw a picture.

The pizza looks delicious.

La pizza se ve deliciosa.

The waiter is serving steaming hot pizza.

El camarero está sirviendo pizza caliente al vapor.

Name

I Can...

- [ ] read the 1st sentence.
- [ ] read the 2nd sentence.
- [ ] make a sentence from a picture.
- [ ] color a picture.
- [ ] Draw a picture.

That is my dad's computer.

Esa es la computadora de mi papá.

My dad works on the computer.

Mi papá trabaja en la computadora.

Name 

I Can...

- [ ] read the 1st sentence.
- [ ] read the 2nd sentence.
- [ ] make a sentence from a picture.
- [ ] color a picture.
- [ ] Draw a picture.

The farmer has a beard.

El granjero tiene barba.

The gardener is going to plant flowers

El jardinero va a plantar flores.

Name

I Can...

- [ ] read the 1st sentence.
- [ ] read the 2nd sentence.
- [ ] make a sentence from a picture.
- [ ] color a picture.
- [ ] Draw a picture.

The strawberry is red.

La fresa es roja.

I love to drink strawberry juice.

Me encanta beber jugo de fresa.

Name

I Can...

- ☐ read the 1st sentence.
- ☐ read the 2nd sentence.
- ☐ make a sentence from a picture.
- ☐ color a picture.
- ☐ Draw a picture.

The magician has a wand.

El mago tiene una varita.

The wizard likes to work with magic.

Al mago le gusta trabajar con magia.

Name

I Can...

- [ ] read the 1st sentence.
- [ ] read the 2nd sentence.
- [ ] make a sentence from a picture.
- [ ] color a picture.
- [ ] Draw a picture.

Reindeer has a scarf.

El reno tiene una bufanda.

Santa gave reindeer a big present.

Santa le dio a los renos un gran regalo.

Name

I Can...

- [ ] read the 1st sentence.
- [ ] read the 2nd sentence.
- [ ] make a sentence from a picture.
- [ ] color a picture.
- [ ] Draw a picture.

I have a lot of pencils.

Tengo muchos lapices.

____

I have a lot of brushes and pencils.

Tengo muchos pinceles y lápices.

Name

I Can...

- [ ] read the 1st sentence.
- [ ] read the 2nd sentence.
- [ ] make a sentence from a picture.
- [ ] color a picture.
- [ ] Draw a picture.

Santa is fat.

Santa es gordo.

Santa is having fun.

Santa se está divirtiendo.

Name

I Can...

- [ ] read the 1st sentence.
- [ ] read the 2nd sentence.
- [ ] make a sentence from a picture.
- [ ] color a picture.
- [ ] Draw a picture.

I have one nose.

Tengo una nariz

The one is saying its name.

El uno está diciendo su nombre.

I Can...

- [ ] read the 1st sentence.
- [ ] read the 2nd sentence.
- [ ] make a sentence from a picture.
- [ ] color a picture.
- [ ] Draw a picture.

I have two ears.

Tengo dos orejas

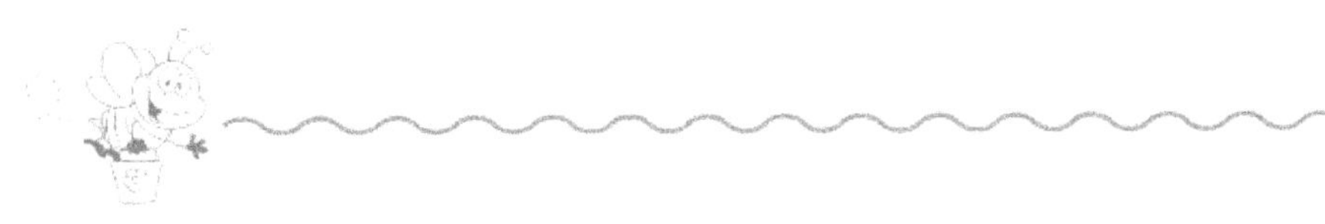

The number "two" is holding up bunny ears.

El número "dos" está sosteniendo orejas de conejo.

Name

I Can...

- [ ] read the 1st sentence.
- [ ] read the 2nd sentence.
- [ ] make a sentence from a picture.
- [ ] color a picture.
- [ ] Draw a picture.

I have three buttons on my dress.

Tengo tres botones en mi vestido.

The number "three" is saying you got 3 out of 3.

El número "tres" dice que obtuviste 3 de 3.

Name

I Can...

- [ ] read the 1st sentence.
- [ ] read the 2nd sentence.
- [ ] make a sentence from a picture.
- [ ] color a picture.
- [ ] Draw a picture.

I have 0 tails.

Tengo 0 colas.

The number "zero" is saying, Ok.

El número "cero" dice: Ok.

Name ____________________

I Can...

- [ ] read the 1st sentence.
- [ ] read the 2nd sentence.
- [ ] make a sentence from a picture.
- [ ] color a picture.
- [ ] Draw a picture.

I have five fingers on 1 of my hands.

Tengo cinco dedos en 1 de mis manos.

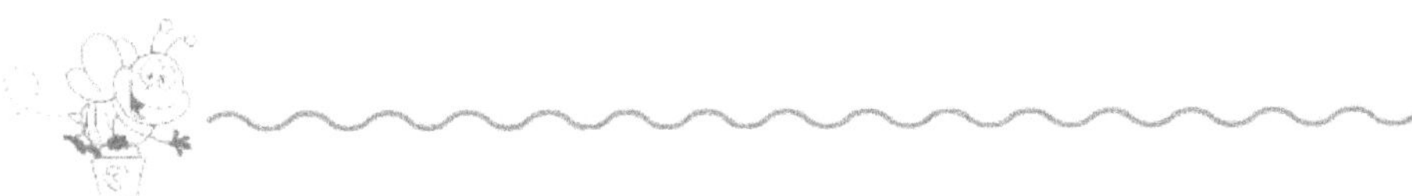

The number "five" is trying to give you a high five.

El número "cinco" está tratando de darte un máximo de cinco.

Name

I Can...

- [ ] read the 1st sentence.
- [ ] read the 2nd sentence.
- [ ] make a sentence from a picture.
- [ ] color a picture.
- [ ] Draw a picture.

My cat has four legs.

Mi gato tiene cuatro patas.

The number "four" is counting to four.

El número "cuatro" cuenta hasta cuatro.

Name

I Can...

- [ ] read the 1st sentence.
- [ ] read the 2nd sentence.
- [ ] make a sentence from a picture.
- [ ] color a picture.
- [ ] Draw a picture.

A butterfly has six legs.

Una mariposa tiene seis patas.

The number "six" is saying 1+5=6.

El número "seis" dice 1 + 5 = 6.

I Can...

- [ ] read the 1st sentence.
- [ ] read the 2nd sentence.
- [ ] make a sentence from a picture.
- [ ] color a picture.
- [ ] Draw a picture.

A spider has eight legs.

Una araña tiene ocho patas.

The happy and excited eight is holding up eight fingers

El feliz y emocionado ocho está levantando ocho dedos

Name

I Can...

- [ ] read the 1st sentence.
- [ ] read the 2nd sentence.
- [ ] make a sentence from a picture.
- [ ] color a picture.
- [ ] Draw a picture.

The rooster is going to wake people up.

El gallo despertará a la gente.

The rooster is on the fence.

El gallo está en la cerca.

Name ______________________

I Can...

- [ ] read the 1st sentence.
- [ ] read the 2nd sentence.
- [ ] make a sentence from a picture.
- [ ] color a picture.
- [ ] Draw a picture.

My sister has nine stuffed animals.

Mi hermana tiene nueve animales de peluche.

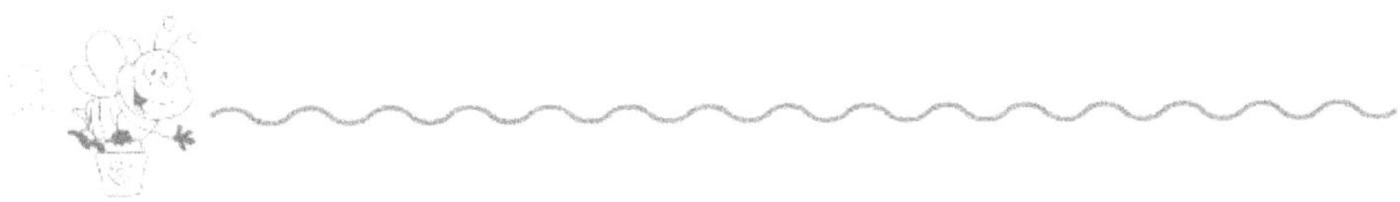

The smiling number nine is saying its name out loud.

El sonriente número nueve dice su nombre en voz alta.

Name 

I Can...

- [ ] read the 1st sentence.
- [ ] read the 2nd sentence.
- [ ] make a sentence from a picture.
- [ ] color a picture.
- [ ] Draw a picture.

The baby bee has yellow and black stripes.

La abeja bebé tiene rayas amarillas y negras.

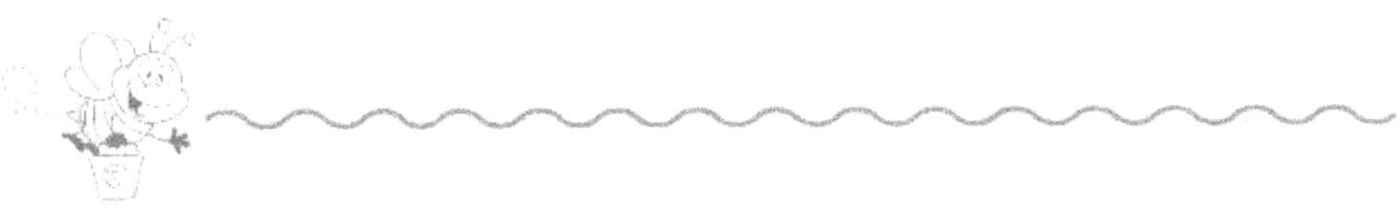

The bee is wearing a pink pacifier to calm itself.

La abeja lleva un chupete rosa para calmarse.

Name

I Can...

- [ ] read the 1st sentence.
- [ ] read the 2nd sentence.
- [ ] make a sentence from a picture.
- [ ] color a picture.
- [ ] Draw a picture.

The ladybug has many spots.

La mariquita tiene muchos puntos.

The red and black ladybug is just done eating some leaves.

La mariquita roja y negra acaba de comer algunas hojas.

Name 

I Can...

- [ ] read the 1st sentence.
- [ ] read the 2nd sentence.
- [ ] make a sentence from a picture.
- [ ] color a picture.
- [ ] Draw a picture.

The sheep are skinny.

Las ovejas son flacas.

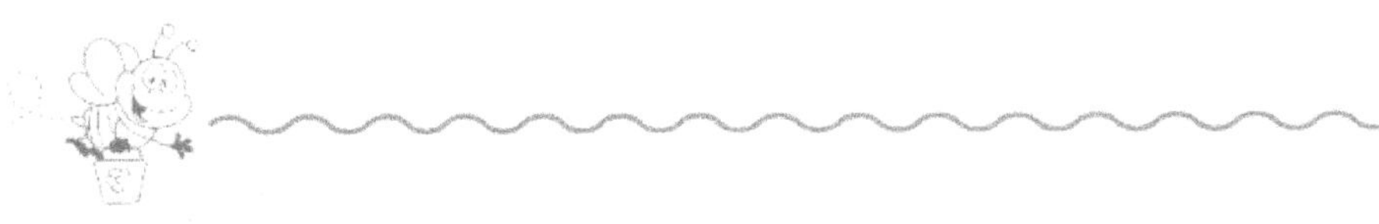

The white sheep have a lot of fluffy white wool to give away.

Las ovejas blancas tienen mucha lana blanca esponjosa para regalar.

Name

I Can...

- [ ] read the 1st sentence.
- [ ] read the 2nd sentence.
- [ ] make a sentence from a picture.
- [ ] color a picture.
- [ ] Draw a picture.

The rabbit is entering an egg painting contest.

El conejo está entrando en un concurso de pintura de huevos.

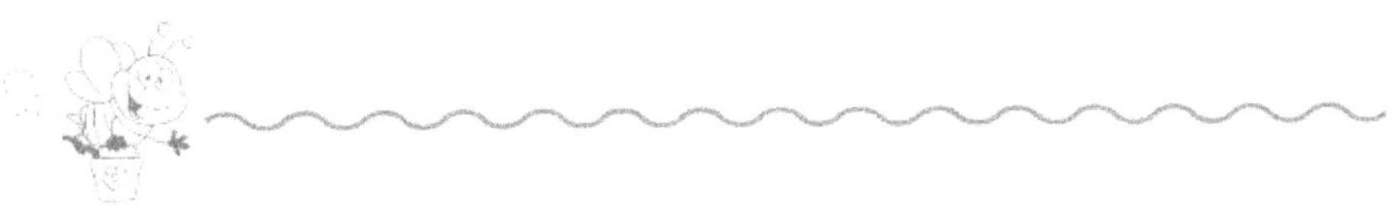

The Easter Bunny is painting a chocolate egg.

El conejito de pascua está pintando un huevo de chocolate.

Name 

I Can...

- [ ] read the 1st sentence.
- [ ] read the 2nd sentence.
- [ ] make a sentence from a picture.
- [ ] color a picture.
- [ ] Draw a picture.

The owl is a language arts teacher.

La lechuza es profesora de artes del lenguaje.

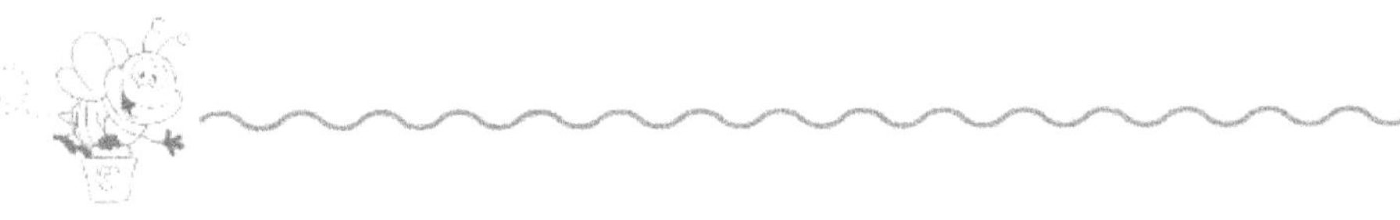

An owl is teaching the kids in school about work.

Una lechuza está enseñando a los niños en la escuela sobre el trabajo.

Name

I Can...

- [ ] read the 1st sentence.
- [ ] read the 2nd sentence.
- [ ] make a sentence from a picture.
- [ ] color a picture.
- [ ] Draw a picture.

The man has an ancient hammer.

El hombre tiene un antiguo martillo.

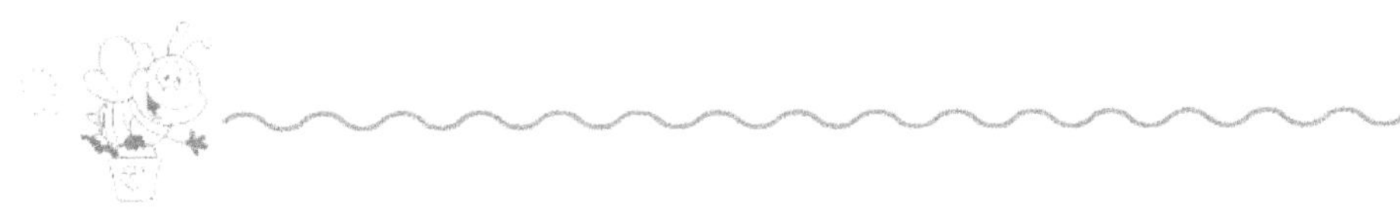

The builder man has gone to work on a project.

El constructor se ha ido a trabajar en un proyecto.

Name

I Can...

- [ ] read the 1st sentence.
- [ ] read the 2nd sentence.
- [ ] make a sentence from a picture.
- [ ] color a picture.
- [ ] Draw a picture.

The goat has a friend.

La cabra tiene un amigo.

The old goat is proud of its golden bell.

La vieja cabra está orgullosa de su campana dorada.

Name

I Can...

- ☐ read the 1st sentence.
- ☐ read the 2nd sentence.
- ☐ make a sentence from a picture.
- ☐ color a picture.
- ☐ Draw a picture.

My mom's friend is a maid.

La amiga de mi madre es una criada.

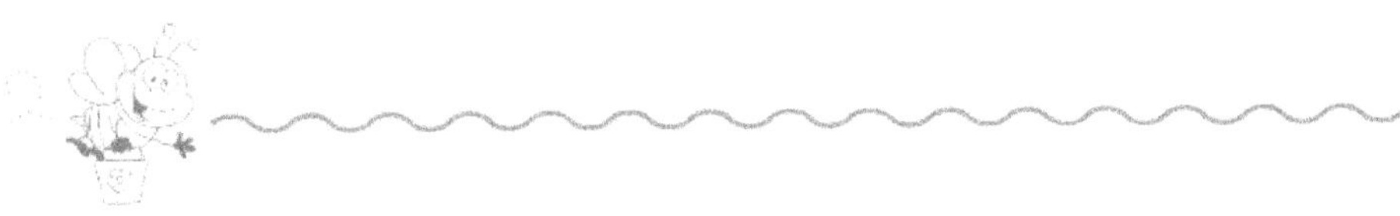

The maid is going to clean the hotel room.

La criada va a limpiar la habitación del hotel.

Name ___________

I Can...

- [ ] read the 1st sentence.
- [ ] read the 2nd sentence.
- [ ] make a sentence from a picture.
- [ ] color a picture.
- [ ] Draw a picture.

I went to the zoo.

Fui al zoológico.

The animals are having a big celebration.

Los animales están teniendo una gran celebración.

Name

I Can...

- [ ] read the 1st sentence.
- [ ] read the 2nd sentence.
- [ ] make a sentence from a picture.
- [ ] color a picture.
- [ ] Draw a picture.

The dinosaur has a pillow.

El dinosaurio tiene una almohada.

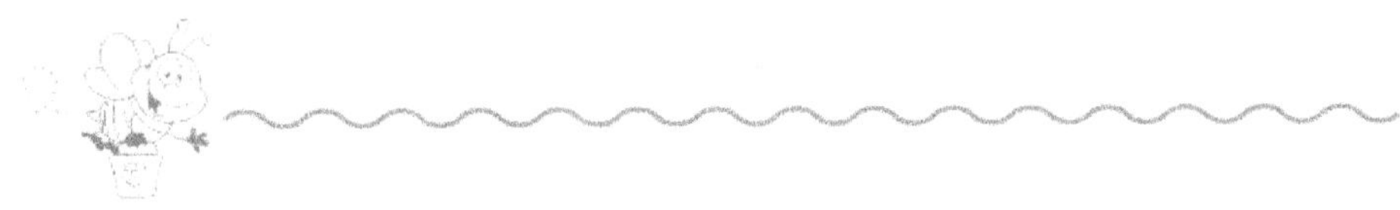

The dragon is using the rock to build its house.

El dragón está usando la roca para construir su casa.

Name

I Can...

- [ ] read the 1st sentence.
- [ ] read the 2nd sentence.
- [ ] make a sentence from a picture.
- [ ] color a picture.
- [ ] Draw a picture.

The boy is excited to go to school.

El niño está emocionado de ir a la escuela.

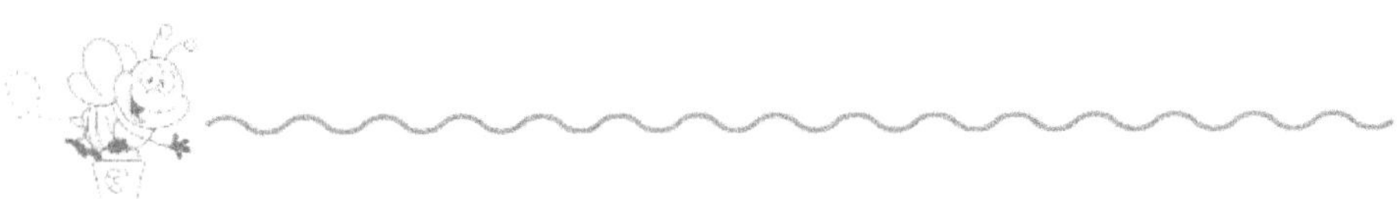

The boy is late for school, so he is sprinting.

El niño llega tarde a la escuela, por lo que está corriendo.

Name ___________

I Can...

- [ ] read the 1st sentence.
- [ ] read the 2nd sentence.
- [ ] make a sentence from a picture.
- [ ] color a picture.
- [ ] Draw a picture.

The kids on the school bus are going to school.

Los niños en el autobús escolar van a la escuela.

The children are going on a field trip on the yellow bus.

Los niños van a una excursión en el autobús amarillo.

Name

I Can...

- [ ] read the 1st sentence.
- [ ] read the 2nd sentence.
- [ ] make a sentence from a picture.
- [ ] color a picture.
- [ ] Draw a picture.

The cobra is very lovely.

La cobra es muy encantadora.

The rattlesnake is looking for its dinner.

La serpiente de cascabel está buscando su cena.

Name

I Can...

- [ ] read the 1st sentence.
- [ ] read the 2nd sentence.
- [ ] make a sentence from a picture.
- [ ] color a picture.
- [ ] Draw a picture.

That is a fat dog!

¡Ese es un perro gordo!

This dog is wagging its tail for more treats.

Este perro está moviendo la cola para más golosinas.

Name

I Can...

- [ ] read the 1st sentence.
- [ ] read the 2nd sentence.
- [ ] make a sentence from a picture.
- [ ] color a picture.
- [ ] Draw a picture.

The elephant lives in the zoo.

El elefante vive en el zoológico.

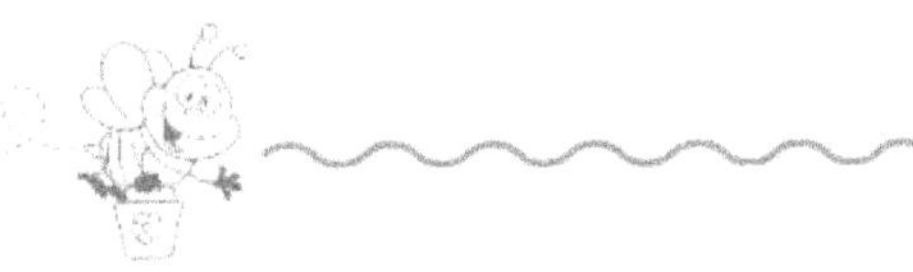

The elephant has a long trunk to spray water.

El elefante tiene una trompa larga para rociar agua.

I Can...

- [ ] read the 1st sentence.
- [ ] read the 2nd sentence.
- [ ] make a sentence from a picture.
- [ ] color a picture.
- [ ] Draw a picture.

The giraffe eats vegetables.

La jirafa come verduras.

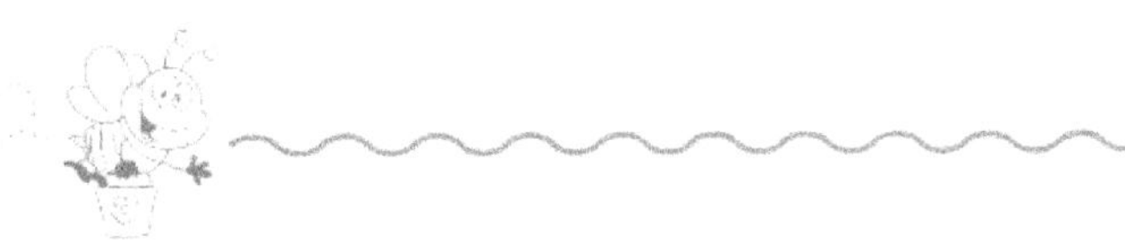

The giraffe has an extremely long neck.

La jirafa tiene un cuello extremadamente largo.

Name

I Can...

- [ ] read the 1st sentence.
- [ ] read the 2nd sentence.
- [ ] make a sentence from a picture.
- [ ] color a picture.
- [ ] Draw a picture.

The chipmunk has a soft tummy.

La ardilla tiene una barriga suave.

The Chipmunk is about to eat a brown acorn.

El Chipmunk está a punto de comer una bellota marrón.

Name 

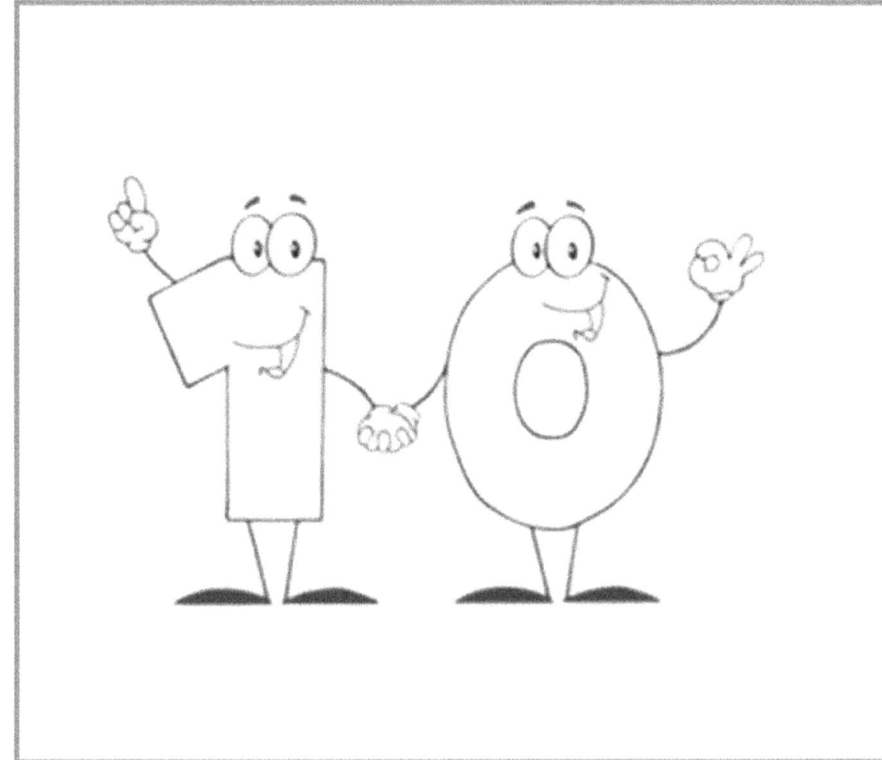

I Can...

- [ ] read the 1st sentence.
- [ ] read the 2nd sentence.
- [ ] make a sentence from a picture.
- [ ] color a picture.
- [ ] Draw a picture.

I have ten toes in total.

Tengo diez dedos en total.

 ________________________________

The one and the zero are holding hands.

El uno y el cero están tomados de la mano.

Name

I Can...

- [ ] read the 1st sentence.
- [ ] read the 2nd sentence.
- [ ] make a sentence from a picture.
- [ ] color a picture.
- [ ] Draw a picture.

The alligator is jumping.

El cocodrilo está saltando.

The crocodile is excited.

El cocodrilo está emocionado.

Name 

I Can...

- [ ] read the 1st sentence.
- [ ] read the 2nd sentence.
- [ ] make a sentence from a picture.
- [ ] color a picture.
- [ ] Draw a picture.

I found an ant.

Encontré una hormiga.

The ant is telling a story.

La hormiga cuenta una historia.

Name

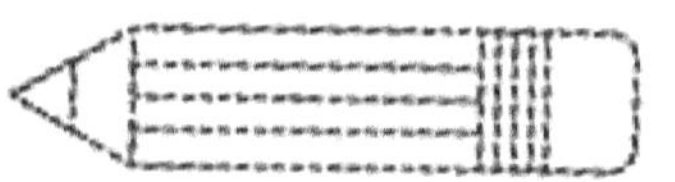

I Can...

- [ ] read the 1st sentence.
- [ ] read the 2nd sentence.
- [ ] make a sentence from a picture.
- [ ] color a picture.
- [ ] Draw a picture.

The bat sleeps upside down.

El murciélago duerme boca abajo.

The bat is ready to fly.

El murciélago está listo para volar.

Name

I Can...

- [ ] read the 1st sentence.
- [ ] read the 2nd sentence.
- [ ] make a sentence from a picture.
- [ ] color a picture.
- [ ] Draw a picture.

The cat is very tired.

El gato está muy cansado.

The cat is taking a nap.

El gato está tomando una siesta.

Name ___________________

I Can...

- [ ] read the 1st sentence.
- [ ] read the 2nd sentence.
- [ ] make a sentence from a picture.
- [ ] color a picture.
- [ ] Draw a picture.

The dog likes to play.

Al perro le gusta jugar.

The dog is playing with a bone.

El perro está jugando con un hueso.

Name

I Can...

- [ ] read the 1st sentence.
- [ ] read the 2nd sentence.
- [ ] make a sentence from a picture.
- [ ] color a picture.
- [ ] Draw a picture.

The elephant has eyelashes.

El elefante tiene pestañas.

The elephant is shy.

El elefante es tímido.

Name

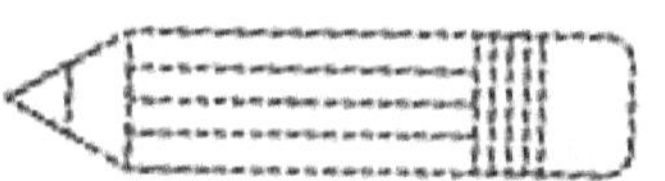

I Can...

- [ ] read the 1st sentence.
- [ ] read the 2nd sentence.
- [ ] make a sentence from a picture.
- [ ] color a picture.
- [ ] Draw a picture.

The frog is hopping.

La rana está saltando.

 ___________________________

The frog is trying to catch the fly.

La rana está tratando de atrapar la mosca.

Name

I Can...

- [ ] read the 1st sentence.
- [ ] read the 2nd sentence.
- [ ] make a sentence from a picture.
- [ ] color a picture.
- [ ] Draw a picture.

The goat is sleepily walking around.

La cabra camina adormilada.

____

The goat is eating grass.

La cabra está comiendo hierba.

Name

I Can...

- ☐ read the 1st sentence.
- ☐ read the 2nd sentence.
- ☐ make a sentence from a picture.
- ☐ color a picture.
- ☐ Draw a picture.

The hippo has a big head.

El hipopótamo tiene una gran cabeza.

The hippo has a big head.

El hipopótamo tiene una gran cabeza.

Name ______________________ 

I Can...

- [ ] read the 1st sentence.
- [ ] read the 2nd sentence.
- [ ] make a sentence from a picture.
- [ ] color a picture.
- [ ] Draw a picture.

The iguana has a long tail.

La iguana tiene una cola larga.

 ~~~~~~~~~~~~~~~~~~~~~~~~~~~~~~~~

The iguana is hiding behind the letter I.

La iguana se esconde detrás de la letra I.

I Can...

- [ ] read the 1st sentence.
- [ ] read the 2nd sentence.
- [ ] make a sentence from a picture.
- [ ] color a picture.
- [ ] Draw a picture.

Mom bought a new bottle of jam.

Mamá compró una nueva botella de mermelada.

 ～～～～～～～～～～～～～～～

There is jam on the bread.

Hay mermelada en el pan.

Name

I Can...

- [ ] read the 1st sentence.
- [ ] read the 2nd sentence.
- [ ] make a sentence from a picture.
- [ ] color a picture.
- [ ] Draw a picture.

The kite has a beautiful tail.

La cometa tiene una hermosa cola.

The kite is on the ground.

La cometa está en el suelo.

Name

I Can...

- [ ] read the 1st sentence.
- [ ] read the 2nd sentence.
- [ ] make a sentence from a picture.
- [ ] color a picture.
- [ ] Draw a picture.

The lion is timid.

El león es tímido

The lion is big.

El leon es grande.

I Can...

- [ ] read the 1st sentence.
- [ ] read the 2nd sentence.
- [ ] make a sentence from a picture.
- [ ] color a picture.
- [ ] Draw a picture.

I like mice.

Me gustan los ratones

A rat is on top of the letter M

Una rata está encima de la letra M

Name

I Can...

- [ ] read the 1st sentence.
- [ ] read the 2nd sentence.
- [ ] make a sentence from a picture.
- [ ] color a picture.
- [ ] Draw a picture.

The nose is breathing.

La nariz está respirando.

The letter N stands for a nose.

La letra N representa una nariz.

Name

I Can...

- [ ] read the 1st sentence.
- [ ] read the 2nd sentence.
- [ ] make a sentence from a picture.
- [ ] color a picture.
- [ ] Draw a picture.

The octopus lives underwater.

El pulpo vive bajo el agua.

The octopus has eight tentacles.

El pulpo tiene ocho tentáculos.

Name

I Can...

- [ ] read the 1st sentence.
- [ ] read the 2nd sentence.
- [ ] make a sentence from a picture.
- [ ] color a picture.
- [ ] Draw a picture.

The penguin eats fish.

El pingüino come pescado.

The penguin lives in the arctic.

El pingüino vive en el ártico.

Name _______________________

I Can...

- ☐ read the 1st sentence.
- ☐ read the 2nd sentence.
- ☐ make a sentence from a picture.
- ☐ color a picture.
- ☐ Draw a picture.

The queen has a wand.

La reina tiene una varita.

____

The queen is beautiful.

La reina es hermosa.

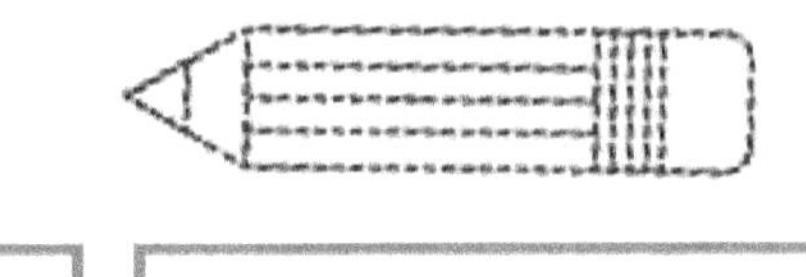

I Can...

- [ ] read the 1st sentence.
- [ ] read the 2nd sentence.
- [ ] make a sentence from a picture.
- [ ] color a picture.
- [ ] Draw a picture.

The rabbit has long ears.

El conejo tiene orejas largas.

The rabbit is thinking about something.

El conejo está pensando en algo.

Name 

I Can...

- [ ] read the 1st sentence.
- [ ] read the 2nd sentence.
- [ ] make a sentence from a picture.
- [ ] color a picture.
- [ ] Draw a picture.

The snake has polka dots.

La serpiente tiene lunares.

 ~~~~~~~~~~~~~~~~~~~~~~~~~~~~~~~~

The snake is licking its lip because it is hungry.

La serpiente se está lamiendo el labio porque tiene hambre.

I Can...

- [ ] read the 1st sentence.
- [ ] read the 2nd sentence.
- [ ] make a sentence from a picture.
- [ ] color a picture.
- [ ] Draw a picture.

The tortoise has a pointy shell.

La tortuga tiene un caparazón puntiagudo.

The turtle has a robust shell but is very slow.

La tortuga tiene un caparazón robusto pero es muy lenta.

Name

I Can...

- [ ] read the 1st sentence.
- [ ] read the 2nd sentence.
- [ ] make a sentence from a picture.
- [ ] color a picture.
- [ ] Draw a picture.

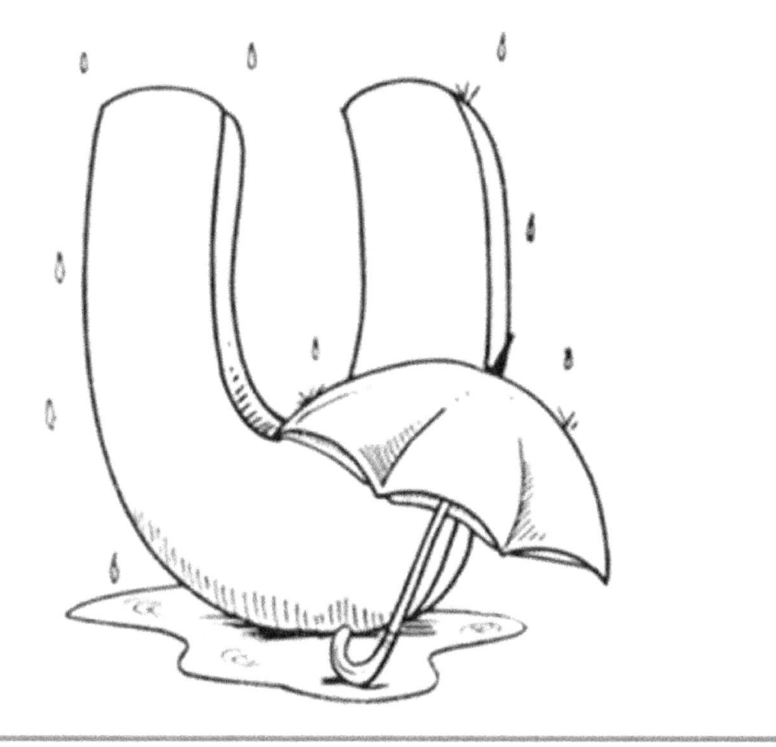

It's raining.

Está lloviendo.

We use the umbrella when it's raining.

Usamos el paraguas cuando está lloviendo.

The violin is a musical instrument.

El violín es un instrumento musical.

A violin can play beautiful music if played correctly.

Un violín puede tocar música hermosa si se toca correctamente.

Name

I Can...

- [ ] read the 1st sentence.
- [ ] read the 2nd sentence.
- [ ] make a sentence from a picture.
- [ ] color a picture.
- [ ] Draw a picture.

The walrus has a friend.

La morsa tiene un amigo.

The walrus has unusually sharp teeth.

La morsa tiene dientes inusualmente afilados.

Name 

I Can...

- [ ] read the 1st sentence.
- [ ] read the 2nd sentence.
- [ ] make a sentence from a picture.
- [ ] color a picture.
- [ ] Draw a picture.

The xylophone is a colorful instrument.

El xilófono es un instrumento colorido.

The xylophone is an instrument like the piano.

El xilófono es un instrumento como el piano.

Name

I Can...

- [ ] read the 1st sentence.
- [ ] read the 2nd sentence.
- [ ] make a sentence from a picture.
- [ ] color a picture.
- [ ] Draw a picture.

The boy has a little hat.

El niño tiene un sombrerito.

____

The boy is having fun playing with a yoyo.

El niño se divierte jugando con un yoyo.

Name

I Can...

- [ ] read the 1st sentence.
- [ ] read the 2nd sentence.
- [ ] make a sentence from a picture.
- [ ] color a picture.
- [ ] Draw a picture.

The zebra has a tail.

La cebra tiene cola.

The zebra has black and white stripes.

La cebra tiene rayas blancas y negras.

Name

I Can...

- [ ] read the 1st sentence.
- [ ] read the 2nd sentence.
- [ ] make a sentence from a picture.
- [ ] color a picture.
- [ ] Draw a picture.

I have a candle on my cake.

Tengo una vela en mi pastel.

I had a small birthday cake for my party.

Tuve un pequeño pastel de cumpleaños para mi fiesta.

Name ________________________ 

I Can...

- [ ] read the 1st sentence.
- [ ] read the 2nd sentence.
- [ ] make a sentence from a picture.
- [ ] color a picture.
- [ ] Draw a picture.

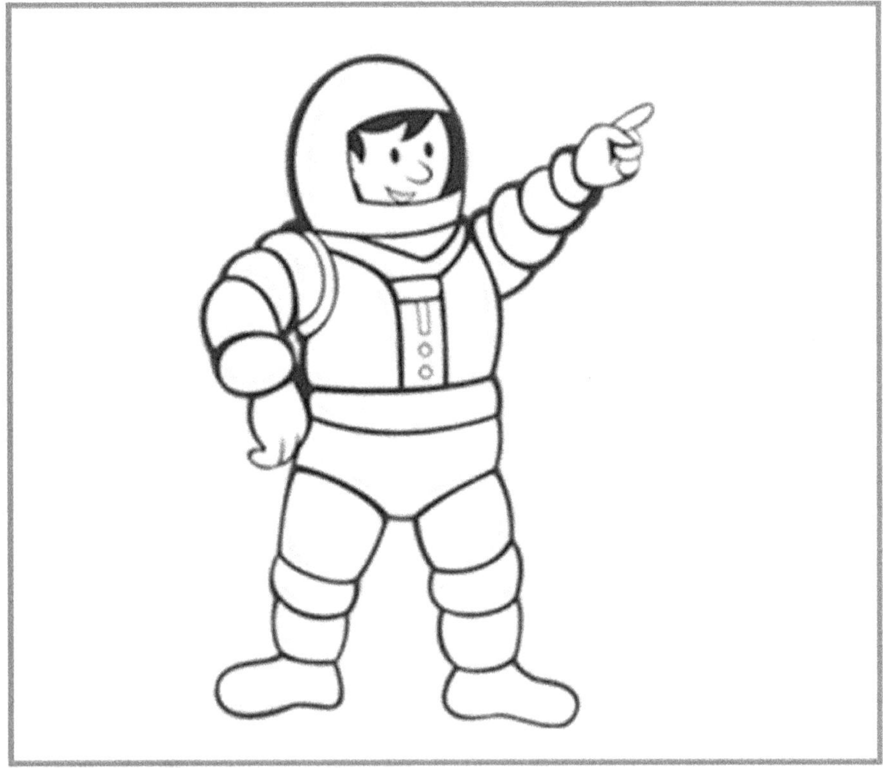

The astronaut is going on a mission.

El astronauta va a una misión.

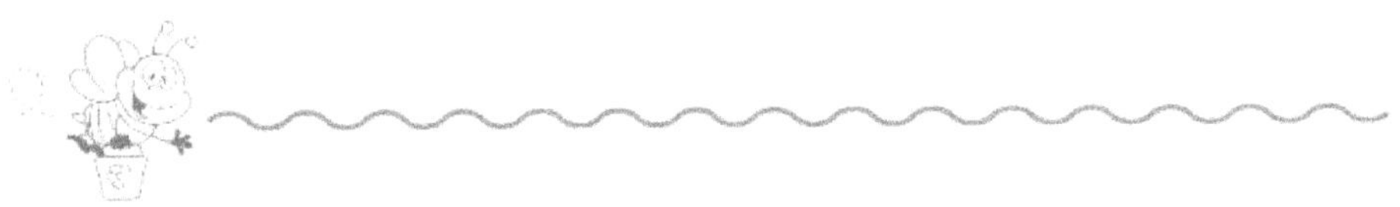

An astronaut has to explore our universe so that we would have more knowledge.

Un astronauta tiene que explorar nuestro universo para que tengamos más conocimiento.

Name

I Can...

- ☐ read the 1st sentence.
- ☐ read the 2nd sentence.
- ☐ make a sentence from a picture.
- ☐ color a picture.
- ☐ Draw a picture.

The samurai is going for a morning jog.

El samurai va a correr por la mañana.

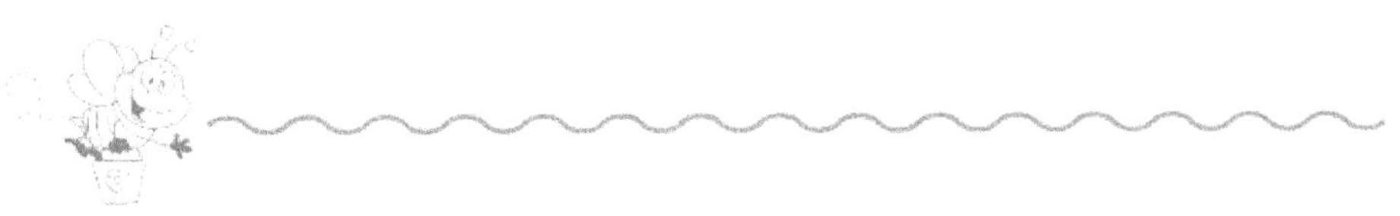

The samurai is training to become good at fighting.

El samurai está entrenando para ser bueno luchando.

Name

I Can...

- [ ] read the 1st sentence.
- [ ] read the 2nd sentence.
- [ ] make a sentence from a picture.
- [ ] color a picture.
- [ ] Draw a picture.

My friend is having a gigantic cake.

Mi amigo está teniendo un pastel gigante.

I had a humongous birthday cake for my celebration.

Tuve un enorme pastel de cumpleaños para mi celebración.

Name

I Can...

- [ ] read the 1st sentence.
- [ ] read the 2nd sentence.
- [ ] make a sentence from a picture.
- [ ] color a picture.
- [ ] Draw a picture.

The frog is chasing the fly.

La rana persigue a la mosca.

The green frog is trying to catch the fly.

La rana verde está tratando de atrapar la mosca.

Name

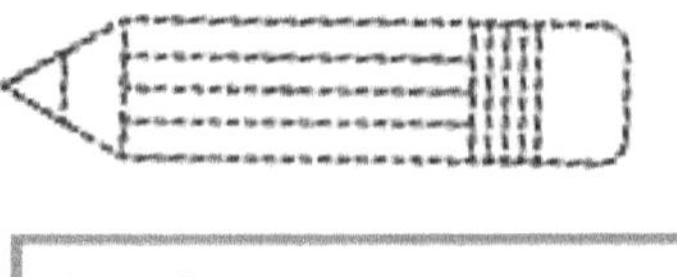

I Can...

- [ ] read the 1st sentence.
- [ ] read the 2nd sentence.
- [ ] make a sentence from a picture.
- [ ] color a picture.
- [ ] Draw a picture.

The ladybug has six legs.

La mariquita tiene seis patas.

The ladybug is on the leaf.

La mariquita está en la hoja.

Name

I Can...

- ☐ read the 1st sentence.
- ☐ read the 2nd sentence.
- ☐ make a sentence from a picture.
- ☐ color a picture.
- ☐ Draw a picture.

The dragon is sick.

El dragón esta enfermo.

The dragon just ate something spicy, so he needed water.

El dragón acaba de comer algo picante, por lo que necesitaba agua.

Name ____________________

I Can...

- ☐ read the 1st sentence.
- ☐ read the 2nd sentence.
- ☐ make a sentence from a picture.
- ☐ color a picture.
- ☐ Draw a picture.

That is a baby cow.

Esa es una vaca bebé.

 ~~~~~~~~~~~~~~~~~~~~~~~~~~~~~~~~~~

A little cow is walking around near the barn.

Una vaca pequeña camina cerca del granero.

Name

I Can...

- [ ] read the 1st sentence.
- [ ] read the 2nd sentence.
- [ ] make a sentence from a picture.
- [ ] color a picture.
- [ ] Draw a picture.

The frog has a big smile.

La rana tiene una gran sonrisa.

 ~~~~~~

The frog is smiling because it is happy.

La rana está sonriendo porque está feliz.

Name ___________________

I Can...

- [ ] read the 1st sentence.
- [ ] read the 2nd sentence.
- [ ] make a sentence from a picture.
- [ ] color a picture.
- [ ] Draw a picture.

The frog has a big mouth.

La rana tiene una boca grande.

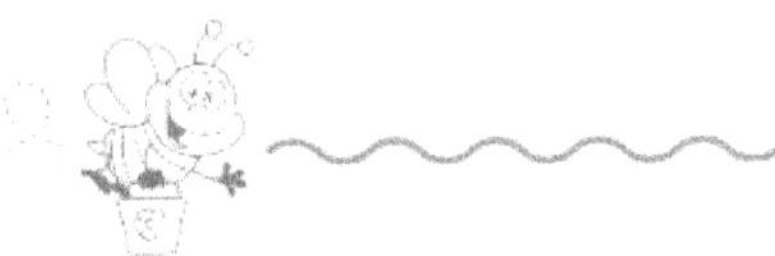 〜〜〜〜〜〜〜〜〜〜〜〜〜〜〜〜〜

The frog is waving to us.

La rana nos saluda.